# THE
# WORST-CASE
# SCENARIO®
## POCKET GUIDE

# DRIVING

**By David Borgenicht**
**and Ben H. Winters**
**Illustrations by Mike Rogalski/Eyewash**

**QUIRK BOOKS**
PHILADELPHIA

Library of Congress Control Number: 2025934204

ISBN: 978-1-68369-527-1

Printed in China

Cover design by Faceout Studio, Spencer Fuller
Typeset by Faceout Studio, Paul Nielsen
Designed by Faceout Studio, based on a design by Liam Flanagan
Interior illustrations by Mike Rogalski/Eyewash
Production management by Mandy Sampson

Quirk Books
215 Church Street
Philadelphia, PA 19106
quirkbooks.com

Quirk Books' authorized representative in the EU for product safety and compliance is Easy Access System Europe, Mustamäe tee 50, 10621 Tallinn, Estonia, gpsr.requests@easproject.com.

10 9 8 7 6 5 4 3 2 1

**WARNING:** You really should have been more careful. Now you're facing one of the worst-case scenarios presented in this book—at least you have the book with you, to refer to. But you must use your good judgment and common sense and consult a professionally trained expert to deal with these dangerous situations. The authors, publisher, and experts disclaim any liability from any injury that may result from the use, proper or improper, from the information contained in this book. Nothing herein should be construed or interpreted to infringe on the rights of other persons or to violate criminal statutes. We urge you to be respectful and safe.

FSC
www.fsc.org
MIX
Paper | Supporting
responsible forestry
FSC® C016973

# CONTENTS

# INTRODUCTION

There's just something about the open road: the wind in your hair, the radio pumping, the sheer unalloyed terror of realizing you're sitting behind the wheel of a giant, steel death machine, hurtling down the highway with nothing but your own split-second reflexes, the questionable abilities of your fellow drivers, and your vehicle's out-of-warranty safety systems standing between you and your own doom.

Let's not kid around here: cars really ought to be called worst-case scenarios on wheels. From the sweating panic of that very first driver's test, cars and the scary situations they inspire are a staple of modern life. When you're not dealing with an engine that's caught fire, you're facing a sudden brake failure, or driving down a flight of stairs to get away from the guy who's chasing you.

Whether it's driving in hurricane or whiteout conditions, bailing out at high speeds, escaping from the trunk of a car, or steering a big rig over the ice roads, you just never know what's coming at you around the next turn. Lucky for you, every one of those situations is covered in this little book, and plenty more besides. So next time you get behind the wheel, make sure you've got *The Worst-Case Scenario Pocket Guide: Driving* (right along with the 22 other items never to leave home without, listed on page 16). It might just save your life—or at least keep you from peeing your pants before the next rest stop (page 21). Either way, we hope you enjoy the ride.

—The Authors

You never really learn to swear
until you learn to drive.

**–Anonymous**

# ROADBLOCKS

# HOW TO SURVIVE BEING STRANDED IN THE SNOW

**1** **Get as far off the road as possible.**

Drive or push your vehicle fully clear of the roadway, but be sure that your car is still visible to any vehicles that may pass by and be able to offer assistance.

**2** **Make your car visible to potential rescuers.**

Turn on your emergency flashers. When the snow stops falling, raise the car's hood to signal distress; when snow begins to fall again, close the hood. Set up flares along the roadside between your car and the road. Hang a brightly colored cloth such as a red scarf or a torn-off piece of blanket from the antenna.

**3** ## Spell out HELP in the snow.

Use rocks and sticks to spell the word HELP in six-foot-long block letters next to the car so your position is visible from the air.

**4** ## Stay near the car.

Do not leave the vicinity of your vehicle unless help is visible within 100 yards. Blowing and drifting snow can be extremely disorienting, causing you to wander away from your car deeper into the snow and become lost. Shelter is your most important priority in inclement weather.

**5** ## Put on all available clothing.

If traveling with clothes, put them on in layers. Wrap yourself in blankets stored in the trunk. Strip the leather or vinyl from your seats and wrap yourself in them.

*Spell out HELP in the snow
with rocks and sticks.*

**6**  **Run the engine for 10 minutes once an hour.**

Clear snow from the exhaust pipe and crack one upwind window to keep carbon monoxide from building up in the car. While the engine is running, turn on the heater to keep body temperature above 90 degrees, warding off hypothermia and frostbite.

**7**  **Remain active.**

While sitting in the car, periodically rotate your torso from side to side and move your arms and legs to keep blood flow moving.

**8**  **Huddle for warmth.**

If traveling with others, sit in a row in the backseat, wrapping your arms and legs together to stay warm. Take turns sleeping.

**9  Forage.**

If the snow stops, walk 50 yards along the shoulder in either direction of your car in search of water, cast-off fast food containers, edible plants, or roadkill. Never let your vehicle out of sight.

**10  Eat snow.**

Keep hydrated by eating chunks of the cleanest snow you can find.

**11  Build a tire signal fire.**

Remove the spare tire from the trunk, or remove one tire from the wheel of the car using a tire jack. Set the tire on the roadway or on a cleared patch of ground near the road. Fill up the center of the tire with dry sticks and paper products from your car and ignite it with the car's cigarette lighter or any other means of ignition. Keep the fire burning with paper products until the fire achieves the 400 degrees necessary to ignite the tire itself. Once lit, a tire will produce a thick black smoke. Do not inhale the smoke, as it contains carbon monoxide, sulfur dioxide, and numerous other toxic chemicals.

## BE AWARE

▶ Symptoms of carbon monoxide poisoning include chest tightness, fatigue, dizziness, vomiting, and muscle weakness.

▶ If afflicted with hypothermia or frostbite, do not drink caffeine or alcohol. Caffeine will amplify the negative effects of cold on the body, while alcohol can slow the heart and restrict blood flow.

▶ Before setting out in winter conditions, stock your trunk with snow chains, bottled water, food, blankets, and signal flares.

▶ Only burn your tires if you have exhausted every effort to restart your vehicle, and no vehicles have come by in 48 hours.

# JUNK IN THE TRUNK: EMERGENCY ITEMS

- Local map, atlas, or GPS system
- Crank or battery-powered radio and batteries
- Large flashlight and batteries
- Matches or lighter
- Basic automotive tool kit
- First-aid kit
- Emergency flares
- Spare tire and jack
- Jumper cables
- 3 days worth of nonperishable food
- 6 quarts of water per adult passenger
- Duct tape
- Pepper spray, emergency whistle
- Collapsible shovel
- Ice scraper, rock salt (for cold weather)
- Insulated sleeping bag
- 2 two-by-fours
- Rain poncho and boots
- License and registration
- Phone charger
- Roadside assistance phone number
- Car owner's manual

# HOW TO BRACE FOR IMPACT

**1** **Stay in control until the last possible moment.**

Keep your hands on the wheel and continue efforts to steer and avoid the obstacle until all options are exhausted.

**2** **Perform a seatbelt check.**

Tug quickly on the lap and shoulder of your belt to make sure you are clicked in and the belt is fully tightened.

**3** **Lean back.**

Move your body fully back in your seat and lay your head against the headrest.

*Hold onto your seatbelt, lift your feet off the pedals, and close your eyes*

**4** **Release the wheel.**

Take your hands off of the steering wheel. At the moment of impact, the wheel may jerk violently, transmitting the shock to your body and breaking your fingers and thumbs.

**5** **Hang onto your seatbelt.**

Clutch the seatbelt with both hands near the place where the lap belt connects to the shoulder belt, so both hands are secure and out of the way of the deploying front and side airbags.

**6** **Lift your feet off the pedals.**

Remove your feet from both the brake and accelerator pedals to avoid having your ankles and shins crushed on impact.

**7** **Close your eyes.**

Protect your vision by closing your eyes tightly. Most cars have shatter-resistant glass, but it may not hold together in certain impacts.

# MOST COMMON FATAL CRASHES

| Type of Crash | Percent of Overall Accidents | Percent of Fatal Accidents |
|---|---|---|
| Rear Impact | 28% | 7.5% |
| Side Impact | 20% | 25% |
| Stationary Object | 20% | 20% |
| Cyclist or Pedestrian | 18% | 19% |
| Head-On | 10% | 11% |
| Animal | 2% | 0.3% |
| Rollover | 2% | 16% |

# HOW TO PEE IN THE CAR WHILE STUCK IN TRAFFIC

**1  Cover the seat.**

Arching your back to elevate your butt from the seat, completely cover the front seat of the car with paper towels or newspaper.

**2  Find a container.**

Look around the interior of the car for a cup with an open or resealable top, such as a travel mug, to-go cup, or refillable sports bottle. Widen the top of a plastic water bottle with a pocket knife or scissors. Avoid containers with small openings, such as glass bottles or aluminum cans.

*Keep your eyes on the road and maintain a neutral expression.*

**3** **Empty the container.**

Roll down the window and dump the contents of the container outside of the car, careful not to splash adjacent vehicles or passersby.

**4** **Pull down your pants.**

Keeping one hand on the wheel, reach down with your other hand, unbutton, unfasten, or adjust your clothing just enough to expose your nether regions.

**5** **Cradle the container between your legs.**

Angle the opening of the container forward at a 45-degree angle.

**6** **Aim into the top of the container.**

Cover your private parts, and the container, with a sweater or roadmap.

**7** ## Do your business.

While you are urinating, keep your eyes fixed on the road and maintain a neutral facial expression. If you have passengers, turn up the radio to hide the noise of the stream.

**8** ## Readjust your clothing.

Set the container in the car's cupholder and refasten and readjust your clothing as normal.

**9** ## Dump out the contents of the container.

Roll down the window and dump the contents of the container outside of the car, being careful not to splash adjacent vehicles or passersby, or damage the paint on your car.

### BE AWARE

Holding in your urine for extended periods can put you at risk for urinary tract infections and can distend your bladder, leading to an increased urinary frequency in the future.

# INSTANT SOLUTION
## Improvise a Sunshade

*Unroll the driver's side window ½ inch.
Remove your jacket, shirt, or blouse.
Tuck it evenly across the top of the window,
then close the window to hold the garment
in place. Lift the garment for visibility when
changing lanes in that direction.*

# HOW TO PARALLEL PARK A TRACTOR TRAILER

**1** **Pull ahead of the space you want.**

Find a parking space that is one and a half times the length of your truck. (If your truck is 20 feet long, your space should be 30 feet long.) Pull up ahead of the space, leaving at least two arm lengths of space between you and the car or truck next to you.

**2** **Turn on your emergency lights.**

**3** **Back up.**

As you put the truck in reverse, give three short horn blasts to alert anyone on the street behind you.

**4**  **Stop.**

When, in your curbside mirror, you see the front end of your truck's trailer even with the rear bumper of the car or truck in front of your chosen space, brake.

**5**  **Turn the wheel.**

Turn the wheel of the tractor away from the curb as far as possible.

**6**  **Swing out.**

Check for oncoming traffic, and then apply gas, swinging the tractor out into the roadway as you back the trailer into the spot. (The trailer will move in the opposite direction that you are turning the wheel.)

**7**  **Cut back.**

When the back curbside wheel of the trailer hits the curb, stop, turn the wheel all the way in the other direction, and pull forward.

*Swing the tractor out into the roadway as you back the trailer into the spot.*

## **8** Repeat steps 6 and 7.

Check both side mirrors to gauge the position of the trailer. If the mirror's blind spot keeps you from seeing the exact position of the trailer, get out of the truck, walk around, and look. Repeat steps 6 and 7 until the trailer is well into the spot and the tractor is not jutting out into the road. Trailers are not designed to go efficiently in reverse and may need dozens of small adjustments to be navigated properly into the space.

## **9** Double check your curb distance and ramp room.

Maneuver the tractor until it is no further than 18 inches from the curb, and the back end is at least 18 feet from the car or truck behind it, so the ramp can come down and moving trolleys can get in and out. If your distances are insufficient, pull out from the space and start again.

## BE AWARE

▶ The narrower the street, the less room you will have to swing out your tractor in step 6. If you are parking on a two- or three-lane street, without minimal oncoming traffic, leave more space between your truck and the car next to you, and swing out further.

▶ Before attempting to navigate city streets in a moving truck, know the height of your vehicle. When approaching over-hanging tree branches, ease forward very slowly to avoid damage to the truck or tree. Do not drive under low-hanging power lines.

▶ Many municipalities require you to give advance notice to the police department to park a moving truck or other tractor-trailer for even a short period of time.

## INSTANT SOLUTION
### Get a Car out of Sand

*Place floor mats (or wood, if available) under the front tires. Accelerate slowly until tires gain traction, and maintain slow, even speed until the car returns to the roadway.*

# HOW TO DRIVE IN A HURRICANE

- Roll up the windows.

- Turn on your high beams.

- Do not drive next to or behind buses and trucks.

  A strong gust of wind can topple a large vehicle over onto your car. Slow down to allow heavy vehicles such as buses and trucks to get ahead and past you. Do not drive behind buses and trucks, as their tires will kick up large amounts of water from the roadway and send it back into your windshield.

*Fill the trunk of your car with heavy objects for ballast.*

- **Weigh down the car.**

  Fill the trunk of your car with heavy objects such as bricks, lumber, appliances, or debris for ballast, to keep the wind from grabbing and flinging the car.

- **Reduce your speed.**

  Drive at 10 miles per hour or less, keeping alert for flying debris and other cars that have stopped or stalled and are blocking the roadway.

- **Apply the brakes as little as possible.**

  In a heavy downpour, there is a significant chance of hydroplaning as water builds up between your wheels and the road. Slow down by taking your foot off the gas rather than applying the brake, and watch for deep puddles.

- **Drive in the middle lane.**

  Water will pool more in the outer lanes of the roadway.

- **Note protected and unprotected areas, and adjust your speed accordingly.**

  You will be sheltered from the wind when driving in protected areas, such as tunnels. When emerging from the protected area, remember to slow down again.

- **Be alert for standing water.**

  If you cannot see the roadway at the bottom of an area covered by water, do not drive into it. Turn around and find another route. Even if it looks like the water is shallow, there may be hidden pits; water of six inches or higher can cause damage and/or stall your car.

- **Be alert for flash floods.**

  Flash floods occur when there is extremely heavy rainfall over a short period of time. They occur most frequently in low-lying areas, such as narrow canyons and valleys. Do not stay in a flooded car; if your car starts to fill up, get out.

## BE AWARE

Never drive in a tornado. If you are in your car when a tornado approaches, exit your car and lie down on your stomach in a ditch or low-lying area, and cover your face and head with your arms.

# HOW TO DRIVE IN A WHITEOUT

- **Wear sunglasses.**

  Don a pair of ultraviolet-blocking sunglasses to prevent snow blindness as the sun reflects off the snow into your eyes.

- **Turn off your lights.**

  High-beams, and even regular headlights, can reflect back in severe snow and reduce your visibility. Drive using only your parking lights.

- **Maintain maximum visibility.**

  Run the windshield wipers on high to keep the windshield clear; when necessary, pull over and wipe the windshield clean. Remove condensation from the windows and windshield by turning on the air conditioner to dehumidify the car. Do not use the windshield wiper fluid; if it's low quality, it may freeze on the windshield.

- **Look for visual clues.**

  Constantly scan roadway for large objects, such as buildings and telephone poles, that will keep you oriented to the relative position of the horizon line and the roadway.

- **Look for ruts left by other drivers.**

  Whenever possible, find the tracks left by other vehicles and drive in them, rather than trying to find your own path down the roadway.

- **Slow down.**

  Drive a maximum of half the posted speed, keeping at least three car lengths between you and the driver ahead.

- **Do not pass other cars.**

  Stay in your lane. Use the running lights of

cars ahead of you to help guide your way, traveling in the ruts left by their wheels.

- **Brake steadily.**

  Apply brakes only when absolutely necessary. Avoid tapping or slamming on the brakes.

- **Avoid rivulets.**

  Watch for small patches of water or melted or semifrozen ice running across the roadway. Steer around such patches when possible. If you must drive over them, do so slowly.

- **Under-react.**

  If you hit a slick of ice or snow, or appear to be headed for a collision, react slowly to events, as any ice on the road will exaggerate your car's reaction to events.

### BE AWARE

When driving in winter, keep your tank half-full at all times to avoid the risk of freezing the gas line.

## YOU AND YOUR
## FELLOW DRIVERS

# @#$&*%!

# HOW TO EVADE A PURSUER

**ESCAPE METHOD**

**1 Identify the pursuer.**

Note the make, model, color, and any other distinguishing features (including the number of passengers) of the pursuing vehicle to help keep track of it in your escape, especially if it is a common vehicle type.

**2 Drive to a high-traffic environment.**

**3 Weave in and out of lanes.**

Look for gaps between cars and suddenly speed up to shift into the gaps. Do not signal your lane changes.

*Weave in and out of lanes.*
*Do not signal your lane changes.*

**4 Drive fast.**

Stay ahead of the flow of traffic.

**5 Turn frequently and unexpectedly.**

When possible, turn right out of the far left lane, or left out of the far right lane.

**6 Seek cover near large vehicles.**

Get as many large, eyeline-blocking vehicles as possible between you and your pursuer. Ride with one truck or bus in front of you and another behind, and then follow the front vehicle into a turn.

**7 Accelerate through yellow lights.**

When you see a traffic light turn yellow, slow until just before it turns red, then accelerate through the intersection at the last moment. Watch for oncoming traffic.

**8 Pitch your pursuer through a yellow light.**

When you see a traffic light turn yellow, and

your pursuer is slightly behind you but not in your lane, speed up to the light as if you intend to speed through it. At the last second, slam on your brakes and let your pursuer speed through the light. Check for oncoming traffic, and then turn.

## DISABLING METHOD

**1** **Drive normally.**

Do not let on that you know you are being followed.

**2** **Situate your car so that your pursuer is directly behind you.**

If your pursuer is trying to maintain their distance, slow down sufficiently so the traffic between your cars will accelerate to pass you.

**3** **Accelerate gently.**

Once your car is directly in front of your pursuer, accelerate gently to put 20 or 30 feet of road between your vehicles.

**4** **Slam on the brakes and throw the car in reverse.**

**5** **Accelerate backwards into your pursuer's car.**

Striking your pursuer's front bumper going at least 15 miles per hour will cause their airbag to deploy, locking the starter of their vehicle.

**6** **Put the car in drive and accelerate forward.**

Drive away quickly.

# CAN I HAVE YOUR RIDE?

## Most Popular Cars with Thieves

- Hyundai Elantra
- Hyundai Sonata
- Kia Optima
- Chevrolet Silverado
- Kia Soul
- Honda Accord
- Honda Civic
- Kia Forte
- Ford F-150
- Kia Sportage

## Most Popular Cars with Consumers

- Toyota RAV4
- Ford F-150
- Honda CR-V
- Tesla Model Y
- Chevrolet Silverado
- Toyota Camry
- Toyota Corolla
- Nissan Rogue
- Honda Civic
- GMC Sierra

# BAD DRIVING BEHAVIOR

| Acceptable | Questionable | Unacceptable |
|---|---|---|
| Applying lipstick | Applying eyeliner | Giving self pedicure |
| Talking to passengers | Talking on cell phone | Writing and sending email |
| Checking hair in rearview mirror | Combing hair | Shaving |
| Drinking to-go beverage | Eating drive-through meal | Making a sandwich |
| Adjusting tie | Tying tie | Changing shirt |

# HOW TO TELL IF YOUR CAR HAS BEEN TAMPERED WITH

**1** **Examine the ground around your car.**

Get down on all fours and crawl along the ground around your car up to a distance of 25 feet away, looking for small bits of wire or wire insulation, discarded scraps of tape, or puttylike lumps.

**2** **Examine the locks and windows.**

Run a flashlight along the cracks between the doors and the doorframes, looking for small wires. Using a magnifying glass, examine the door locks and windows, and the area directly surrounding them, for scrapes or scratches indicating forced entry. Check the seam around the trunk; open the trunk and make sure the mats have not been moved, and there are no unfamiliar objects or bits of wire or wire insulation.

**3** ## Examine the gas tank.

Run your hands over the crack around the gas tank cover to make sure it is flush and shows no signs of prying. Use a magnifying glass to look for scuff marks or scratches. Open the gas tank cover and sniff the tank for strong, nongas odors.

**4** ## Open the hood.

Shine your flashlight around the engine block, particularly the wiring, to see if anything is disconnected or if there are any new wires present. Run the light along the firewall (the back wall of the engine, separating the fuel tank from the passenger compartment) to make sure it has not been sabotaged.

### **5** **Use a mirror to examine the under-side of the car.**

Slide a small handheld mirror under the chassis and slowly move it clockwise around the underside of the car, examining the reflected image for foreign objects attached to the vehicle.

### **6** **Check your brakes.**

Lie down a foot away from the front of the car and sweep your flashlight underneath it, looking for a puddle of greasy liquid, which may be brake fluid that has been drained from your vehicle. Run one finger slowly along the brake lines, from each brake pad back to the master cylinder, feeling for pin-holes or cuts.

### **7** **Look into the exhaust pipe.**

Shine a flashlight into the pipe to look for foreign objects.

*Shine a flashlight into the pipe
to look for foreign objects.*

**8**  ## Inspect your wheels and tires.

Run your hands all the way around each tire to feel for minor punctures or small slashes. Feel each lug nut to make sure it is still properly tightened. Check the air pressure of each tire with a tire pressure gauge to make sure no one has let the air out of your tires.

**9**  ## Examine the front seats for signs of intrusion.

Before opening the car door, look through the window for signs that someone has been in the car. Note whether the angle of the seats has been altered, if the rearview mirror has been redirected, or if the floor mats have been moved or disturbed.

**10**  ## Take a deep breath.

Once settled in the driver's seat, sniff the air. The odor of gasoline within the vehicle can indicate that the gas tank has been tampered with or punctured.

## **11** Look for a planted device.

Run your fingers along the underside of the passenger and driver's seats in search of foreign objects. Check under the brake and acceleration pedals. Do not apply pressure to the seats until you are satisfied there is nothing beneath them that may be pressure-triggered.

### BE AWARE

▶ The best way to notice any tampering is to know your vehicle well under normal circumstances. Carry a photograph of the inside of your engine so you can check the arrangement of wires against the picture before starting your car each time.

▶ Always leave objects on your front seat, such as newspapers or tissue boxes, so you can gauge whether someone has moved them when you return to the car.

# TOP TEN IN-CAR ACTIVITIES THAT LEAD TO ACCIDENTS

1. Wireless devices (Cell phones, digital assistants, GPS, Bluetooth)
2. In-car communication (Dictating notes-to-self, yelling at children)
3. Internal distractions (Fumbling for dropped phone, looking for items on seat)
4. Grooming (Applying makeup, picking teeth)
5. Dashboard activities (Finding a radio station, adjusting air conditioning)
6. Eating or drinking
7. External distractions (Rubbernecking, checking out attractive person in oncoming vehicle)
8. Singing or talking to yourself
9. Smoking (Reaching for, lighting, putting out cigarettes)
10. Daydreaming

# HOW TO ESCAPE FROM THE TRUNK OF A CAR

**1** **Breathe.**

Resist the urge to panic. Trunks are not air-tight, which means you will probably die of dehydration or overheating before suffocating, but hyperventilating will deplete the store of oxygen more quickly.

**2** **Feel for a safety latch.**

Run your palms slowly and deliberately over every surface of the trunk's interior. The safety latch, if there is one, will most likely be located in the center of the trunk lid. Many car models now come with a safety latch

*Exert downwards force on your sharp
metal object until you pop the latch
and release the trunk.*

preinstalled; in others, the owner may have installed a store-bought model, typically a white plastic handle dangling on a small piece of cord.

### 3 Look for a trunk cable.

Pull up the trunk carpet and search on the driver's side of the car for a cable running from the driver's seat to the trunk. Yank up hard on the cable to pop the trunk.

### 4 Kick out the backseat of the car.

Brace your back against the rear end of the trunk. Using both legs, kick against the center of the wall separating the trunk from the backseat. Kick once at the center and then once at each of the sides, testing each to see if there is any give. If after three strong kicks you do not feel the wall begin to move, preserve your energy and oxygen and move on to the next step.

## **5** Search for tools.

Feel carefully around the floor of the trunk for anything long and metal you can use to jimmy the trunk latch, such as a tire iron, pry bar, or long screwdriver. Look under the trunk carpet for any niches or hidden compartments.

## **6** Jimmy the trunk latch.

Find the trunk latch at the center of the long horizontal crack where the trunk lid meets the base. Jab one end of your sharp metal object at the latch at a 45-degree angle and exert downwards force on the metal object, until you pop the latch and release the trunk.

### BE AWARE

- ► The majority of trunk-entrapments occur in a person's own car. Keep a flashlight and crowbar in your car, or install a glow-in-the-dark release mechanism.

- ► Since 1970, at least 1,250 people have been locked in trunks in the United States, and at least 300 have died.

**DRIVING EXTREMES**

# LOOKS EASIER
# IN THE MOVIES

# HOW TO SURVIVE A BLOWOUT ON THE ICE ROAD

**1  Ride with your hand on the door.**

The first sign of a blowout—a wave of water under the ice that causes a tear in its surface—will be black water seeping through the ice's surface. If black water is visible, move one hand from the steering wheel to the handle of the door.

**2  Speed up.**

Ignore the instinct to brake, which can send the truck into a skid or exacerbate the blow-out by concentrating your weight on the crack. Accelerate by a few miles per hour to carry your weight forward past the crack.

### 3 Jump out.

When the front end of the truck starts to go through the ice, open the door of the cab and leap out.

### 4 Roll.

Upon landing, roll as quickly and as far as possible from the sinking cab.

### 5 Stay put.

Do not wander through the whiteout conditions in search of help, as you can quickly become disoriented. Stay where you are until another vehicle from your convoy can reach you.

## AVOID A BLOWOUT

### 1 Go slow.

Stay below 15 miles per hour to avoid churning up the under-ice waves that lead to blowouts.

*Jump out of the cab.*

**2** ## Do not stop.

Keep your vehicle moving at all times, as the concentrated heat and weight of a stopped truck can cause the surface of the ice to crack.

**3** ## Know where the other drivers are.

Stay in radio and visual contact with the other members of your convoy to avoid a truck-on-truck collision, which will severely damage the ice floor.

### BE AWARE

▶ The ice roads, which can only be driven in the winter when the ice is sufficiently thick, cross the frozen lakes of Canada's Northwest Territories, servicing Canada's diamond mines.

▶ Until the ice is 42 inches thick, which usually happens in mid-February, the ice road cannot reliably bear the 70-ton weight of a fully loaded truck.

- The ice is most fragile closest to the shoreline.

- The sound of ice cracking beneath your rig is not alarming; frozen sheets of ice are constantly breaking and reforming to adjust to weight. If you don't hear cracking, the ice is too thin.

# HERE'S YOUR PROBLEM: WHEN THINGS WEAR OUT

| | |
|---|---|
| Oil Filters | 5,000 to 10,000 miles |
| Power Steering Fluid | 100,000 miles |
| Brake Fluid | 30,000 miles |
| Brake Pads | 10,000 to 30,000 miles |
| Clutch | 75,000 to 100,000 miles |
| Engine | 250,000 to 350,000 miles |
| Taillights | Two to three years |
| Wiper Blades | Six months |
| Battery | Two years |
| Exhaust Systems/ Mufflers | 100,000 miles |
| Shocks and Struts | 100,000 to 150,000 miles |
| Airbags | 10 years |
| Radiators | Five to six years |
| Timing Belt | 60,000 miles to 100,000 miles |

# HOW TO DRIVE DOWN A FLIGHT OF STAIRS

**1  Aim.**

Set your eyes on a spot dead center over the horizon of the staircase, and steer the car toward it.

**2  Floor it.**

When you are twenty feet from the stairs, slam your foot down on the accelerator to get a burst of speed approaching the lip.

**3  Shut your mouth.**

Pull your tongue back in your mouth and grit your teeth to keep them from knocking together as the car bounces down the stairs.

*Floor it.*

**4** ## Grip the wheel.

Hold onto the wheel tightly, and steer to counterbalance each time the car jerks one way or the other as it bounces forward.

**5** ## Lift your foot from the accelerator.

As the front bumper crosses the lip of the top stair, lift up your feet. Further acceleration is unnecessary as gravity pulls your vehicle forward, and leaving your feet on the pedals will cause your shins to absorb the shock as the car bangs down the steps.

**6** ## Floor it again.

When you feel the back wheel hit the bottom stair, bring your right foot back down on the pedal and give another burst of speed to keep your back bumper from catching on the lip of the bottom step.

**7** ## Even out.

Hold tightly to the wheel and steer to regain control of the vehicle.

## HOW TO DRIVE UP A FLIGHT OF STAIRS

**1 Aim and accelerate.**

Check both side mirrors to make sure you are giving adequate space on either side. When you are twenty feet from the bottom stair, give a burst of gas.

**2 Further accelerate as your front wheel hits the first stair.**

Give more gas to take your back wheels up onto the stairs.

**3 Maintain speed as you climb.**

Continue to accelerate as you go up the stairs, to keep gravity from pulling you back down. Give a final burst of speed as you come over the top.

## BE AWARE

▶ If your car is too low to the ground, the underside will be scraped and banged by the stairs all the way up or down, causing serious damage. Fully inflated tires will give you more clearance.

▶ Time permitting, laying down a wooden ramp across the bottom stair will make your approach to the uphill drive easier, and mitigate the effects of low clearance.

▶ A front-wheel drive car will be more effective than a rear-wheel drive car, while an all-wheel drive car is ideal, since the drive system sends more traction to the various tires as needed.

# INSTANT SOLUTION
## Fire Under the Hood

*Pull over and turn off the engine. Do not open the hood. Exit the car and move at least 100 yards from the burning vehicle. Call for emergency assistance.*

# HOW TO SURVIVE A ROLLOVER

**1 Pull your feet off the pedals.**

As the car starts to roll, lift your feet from the brake and accelerator pedals and tuck them under the seat to keep your ankles from breaking against the floor of the vehicle.

**2 Let go of the wheel.**

If you are hanging onto the wheel when the car slams into the ground again, the impact will be transmitted through your entire body. Once the car has begun to roll, turning the wheel will not have any effect.

**3 Cross your arms over your chest.**

Keep your arms and hands as far as possible

from the windows of the car as the window
side slams into the ground.

### 4 Brace yourself with your feet.

Once the car is upside down, find purchase
somewhere with both feet, either on the
windshield, the driver's side window, or on
the ceiling of the car.

### 5 Count to sixty.

Remain still and suspended from your seatbelt until you are certain that your vehicle has
stopped moving, and that any other vehicles
involved in the accident have stopped moving and are not sliding across the roadway into
yours.

### 6 Check yourself for injuries.

While hanging onto the seatbelt with one
hand, pat your body with the other hand to
check for injuries. Run your hand through
your hair and over your scalp. In case of any
injury, do not move.

Support your weight against the
ceiling of the car and unfasten your seatbelt.

**7** **If you appear to be uninjured, reach up and stabilize yourself.**

As you are dangling from the seatbelt, slowly raise one hand and lay it firmly against the ceiling of the car.

**8** **Unfasten your seatbelt.**

When you are certain your weight is fully supported by your hands and feet, un-click your seatbelt and drop down onto the ceiling.

**9** **Get out of the car.**

Check for oncoming traffic. Open the door and exit the vehicle. Get clear of the roadway and await emergency personnel.

**BE AWARE**

▶ Rollovers occur when a driver loses control of the vehicle, it slides sideways, and it hits a "trip," such as a curb or guardrail. A second common cause is a driver taking a turn or curve too quickly.

- Rollovers account for only 3 percent of total accidents, but cause about a quarter of fatal crashes. More than half the people killed in single-vehicle crashes die in rollovers.

- Many rollover injuries occur after the accident itself, when the victim unbuckles their seatbelt and falls to the roof of the car.

- Cars are more prone to rollovers when they have a high center of mass, meaning that pickup trucks, SUVs, and vans are more likely to roll than other passenger cars.

- Always wear your seatbelt.

# THOSE WERE THE DAYS: THE MODEL T VS. THE AVERAGE CAR TODAY

|  | Original Model T | Modern 4-Door Sedan |
|---|---|---|
| **Price** | $850 | $28,400 |
| **Manufacturing Time** | 1 car every 93 minutes | 50 to 60 cars every hour |
| **Cars Sold** | 10,000 (first year) | 16 million annually |
| **Horsepower** | 20 | 170 |
| **Top Speed** | 45 mph | 160 mph |
| **Weight** | 1,200 lbs | 3,300 lbs |
| **Price of a Gallon of Gas** | 7 to 10 cents | $3 to $4 |
| **Miles per Gallon** | 25 | 30 |

# HOW TO BAIL OUT OF A CAR AT HIGH SPEEDS

**1** **Look for the best place to bail out.**

Try to bail out into a body of water or into foliage. Failing that, drive as close to the curbside as possible to avoid leaping into traffic.

**2** **Unbuckle your seatbelt.**

Steer the car with one hand as you unbuckle the seatbelt with the other. Pull the lap and chest belts fully clear of your body to avoid entanglement.

**3** **Tuck your chin.**

Close your mouth tightly and angle your neck down until your chin rests on your breastbone.

*Hold your arms across your chest.*

**4** ## Brace your feet.

Remove both feet from the pedals and place them squarely on the floorboards of the vehicle, in front of the pedals.

**5** ## Open the door.

In one swift movement, grasp the door handle and fling open the door of the vehicle.

**6** ## Spring out of the car.

As soon as the door is completely open, push against the floor of the car with both feet to throw your body upward and outward from the car.

**7** ## Cross your arms.

With each hand, grab the opposite shoulder tightly, keeping your arms across your chest.

**8** ## Land and roll.

As you hit the ground, roll as far from the car as possible, to avoid your rear wheels and other cars.

# DAILY COMMUTE TIMES

| | |
|---|---|
| **Villavicencio, Colombia** | 3 hours 12 minutes |
| **Myrtle Beach, SC, USA** | 1 hour 36 minutes |
| **Sarasota, FL, USA** | 1 hour 26 minutes |
| **Denver, CO, USA** | 47 minutes |
| **Manila, Philippines** | 45.5 minutes |
| **Kuala Muda, Malaysia** | 44.3 minutes |
| **Moscow, Russia** | 43.1 minutes |
| **Jakarta, Indonesia** | 42.1 minutes |
| **Montpellier, France** | 41.2 minutes |
| **London, England** | 41.2 minutes |

# HOW TO STOP A CAR WITH FAULTY BRAKES

**1** **Keep your eyes on the road.**

Until you are able to stop, your most urgent priority is to continue to steer the car.

**2** **Pump brakes.**

Build pressure with remaining brake fluid by pumping the brakes continuously.

**3** **Downshift.**

If you are in a manual transmission car, engage the clutch and downshift; do so again and then again until you are in your transmission's lowest gear. In an automatic transmission car, move the gear shifter to the

*Steer the car into an environment that will do the minimum amount of damage to the car and passengers.*

lowest gear, from drive down to second and then into first.

**4** ## Engage the emergency brake.

Depending on the make and model of your vehicle, the emergency brake may be a hand lever located between the driver and the front passenger or a foot-operated pedal to the left of the regular driving pedals, close to the driver's side door of the vehicle. Pull or step on the emergency brake gently in a steady, constant motion.

**5** ## Drive up a hill.

If driving on the highway, look for an exit ramp that will take you uphill; in the city, turn off the road onto an uphill street. Gravity will slow down your vehicle as you drive up the incline.

**6** ## Seek a soft landing.

Steer the car off the road into an environment that will do the minimum amount of damage to the car and passengers, such as a patch of bushes or a snowy field.

### 7 Scrub off speed.

Drive alongside a wall, guard rail, or the side of a building. Bring the car closer and closer until the side of the car is "kissing" the wall or rail, sending off sparks and slowing down the rate of speed with a series of small collisions.

### 8 Turn off the engine.

As a last resort, turn the car off. The rate of acceleration will rapidly decrease; however, steering becomes impossible.

# I TAKE THAT BACK:

| Year | Nature of problem |
|------|-------------------|
| 1971 | Engine mounts fell off |
| 1971 | Seatbelt decay |
| 1972 | Windshield wipers flew off in storms |
| 1973 | Steering assembly disabled by stones from roadway |
| 1978 | Gas tank subject to explosion |
| 1981 | Suspension bolts came loose, impeding steering |
| 1987 | Engine compartment fires |
| 1996 | Steering column fires |
| 1996 | Ignition systems catch fire |
| 2004 | Defective tailgate cables |
| 2005 | Faulty headlights |
| 2007 | Cruise control switch bursts into flames |
| 2014 | Exploding airbags |

# MAJOR SAFETY RECALLS

| Model(s) | Number of cars affected |
| --- | --- |
| GMs including Camaro, Chevrolet, G Series, Impala, P Series, and C Series | 6.7 million |
| Fords including Ranchero, Lincoln, and Mercury | 4.1 million |
| VW Bugs | 3.7 million |
| GMs including LeSabre, Caprice, and Impala | 3.7 million |
| Ford Pinto | 1.5 million |
| GMs including Century and Malibu | 5.8 million |
| Ford almost all models | 3.6 million |
| Ford various models | 8 million |
| Fords including Escort, Mustang, Thunderbird, and Lincoln Town Car | 8.6 million |
| GMs including Silverado, Sierra, Escalades and Avalanche | 3.6 million |
| Toyota Corollas and others | 1.4 million |
| Fords, including Lincoln and Mercury | 3.6 million |
| Many automakers, including Acura, BMW, Chrysler, and Dodge | 67 million |

# INDEX

# ACKNOWLEDGMENTS

**David Borgenicht** would like to thank Ben Winters, Jess Zimmerman, Andie Reid, Jane Morley, Kassie Andreadis, Mike Rogalski, and Jen Worick for making this book happen. He promises each of you a free oil and filter change at 5,000 miles.

**Ben H. Winters** would like to thank the following automotive experts: Mark Cox at Bridgestone Winter Driving School, Robert Prevost at RacingSchools.com, Mike Burke of Driver's East, trucker A.J. Jones, and the good and safe people at the Insurance Institute of Highway Safety and AAA.

# ABOUT THE AUTHORS

**David Borgenicht** is the creator and coauthor of all the books in the Worst-Case Scenario® series and is president and publisher of Quirk Books (www.quirkbooks.com). He lives in Philadelphia.

**Ben H. Winters** is a *New York Times* best-selling, award-winning novelist and has also worked extensively in television. He lives in Los Angeles with his wife, three kids, and one large dog.

**Mike Rogalski** is an award-winning illustrator who has been surviving deadlines since long before pixels were the preferred medium. His portfolio of published work encompasses a range of subjects including mummy preparation, igloo construction, waste management on the International Space Station, and the internal workings of Snuffleupagus.

# ABOUT WORST-CASE SCENARIO®

Worst-Case Scenario® is the world's best-selling survival brand. Since emerging in 1999, *The Worst-Case Scenario Survival Handbook* has sold more than eleven million copies, been translated into more than two dozen languages, and spawned more than thirty sequels, two television series, board games, card games, a traveling museum exhibition, and much more, providing expert advice for extreme situations, amusing and informing fans, and even saving lives.

Our brand philosophy: Be prepared. Don't panic. Face your fears. Have a plan.

# MORE WORST-CASE SCENARIO® PRODUCTS

For updates, new scenarios, and more stuff, and to order books, visit www.worstcasescenario.com.